CW00815823

THE SLEEPING BEAUTY
OF SAVOY

...and other precious nonsense !

Remembering John King
Who designed and made our wonderful costumes

Published by Cynthia Morey and John Fryatt
Publishing partner: Paragon Publishing, Rothersthorpe
First published 2007
© Cynthia Morey and John Fryatt 2007

The rights of Cynthia Morey and John Fryatt to be identified as authors of this work have been asserted by them in accordance with the Copyright, Designs and Patents Act of 1988.

All rights reserved; no part of this publication may be reproduced, stored in a retrieval system, or transmitted in any form or by any means, electronic, mechanical, photocopying, recording or otherwise without the prior written consent of the publisher or a licence permitting copying in the UK issued by the Copyright Licensing Agency Ltd, 90 Tottenham Court Road, London W1P 9HE.

Condition of Sale

This book is sold subject to the condition that it shall not, by way of trade or otherwise, be lent, resold, hired out or otherwise circulated in any form of binding or cover other than that in which it is published and without a similar condition including this condition being imposed on the subsequent purchaser.

ISBN 978-1-899820-42-9
Book design, layout and production management by Into Print
www.intoprint.net
Printed and bound in UK and USA by Lightning Source

Our Gilbert and Sullivan Pantomime-

and how it came to be written:

John Fryatt and I began our careers in the D'Oyly Carte Opera Company, and later went on to join Sadler's Wells / English National Opera. Although our paths eventually diverged, we always kept in close touch. John mainly continued in opera, world-wide, apart from a stint in Stephen Sondheim's 'Follies' at the Shaftesbury Theatre, while I moved on to West End musicals- among them 'My Fair Lady', 'Fiddler on the Roof', 'Me and My Girl' and 'Anything Goes'.

Loving the Players' Theatre Victorian pantomimes so much, and having both appeared in them, it occurred to us that the delightful characters and music of Gilbert and Sullivan would lend themselves very well to similar treatment. So the idea was born, and we worked on it for some considerable time. As we lived a fair distance apart (this was before e-mails!) many hilarious phone calls ensued, and the most improbable rhymes and impractical ideas were exchanged. Eventually 'The Sleeping Beauty of Savoy' emerged.

Our Pantomime has had three productions: one by the Sale Gilbert and Sullivan Society at the Garrick Playhouse, Altringham, (directed by Roberta Morrell and featuring Alistair Donkin as Mad Meg), one at the Oast Theatre, Tonbridge (directed by Jean Bruce) and one at the Opera House, Buxton, in which John and I played the Wicked and the Good Fairies respectively.

The Oast Theatre production particularly impressed us, and here is director Jean Bruce's account of it in the local press, written soon after the end of the run of twelve performances:

'Choosing the right show is always difficult' were the words which prompted me to write to you regarding a new show premiered in the South, at the Oast Theatre, Tonbridge, last Christmas.

'The Sleeping Beauty of Savoy' was devised and written by Cynthia Morey and John Fryatt, both ex-soloists of the D'Oyly Carte opera Company. it tells the traditional story of the Sleeping Beauty in true Victorian style, using the characters of Sir W.S.Gilbert and Sir Arthur Sullivan.

Although written for a reasonably large company, 'Sleeping Beauty' adapted perfectly to the confines of a small theatre and a total cast of twenty-nine, twelve of these being principals. This meant that the chorus were kept busy being Servants, Fiends and Courtiers, and various characters from the G & S Operas.

Principal characters were the Sleeping Beauty herself (alias Rose Maybud); the nautical King Corcoran; ex-actress Queen Julia; two dandy Lord Chamberlains (Tolloller and Mountararat); the handsome Prince Hilarion; the Fairy Queen and her three scatter-brained Fairies; Royal nursemaid Ruth, and Mad Meg, the wicked Fairy (a Dame role). We were able to introduce some younger chorus members as Rose Maybud's friends, and true to G & S tradition we included a Pageboy (aged three!).

Staging had to be adapted; originally eleven scenes, we decided on a day bed on a plinth, and an impressive double staircase to give a higher level. The 'attic' was at the top of this staircase, with a festoon curtain, raised and lowered for the spinning wheel scene. With this set, a forest gauze, good lighting, and- I hasten to add- good lighting operators and stage staff, we managed to achieve all that was needed. Particularly impressive was the Finale to Act I, where the whole cast is under the spell that makes them sleep for a hundred years, and is set to music from a similar situation in 'The Sorcerer'.

Costumes can be as simple or as impressive as you like. The Queen needs as many changes as the script allows, as she is more concerned about her appearance than she is about her offspring! The King needs a nautical uniform. Princess Rose and her friends we decided to dress in Kate Greenaway style. the Fairy Queen was taken from the original 'Iolanthe' design, and the scatty Fairies stripped to their underwear of corset and bloomers (very demure!)
when they had been on sentry duty for a hundred years. The chorus, when playing guests at the Christening, we dressed as various G & S characters.

We were only able to use piano, double bass and flute as accompaniment, as space was strictly limited; our musical director was playing the piano, so could control the stage from that position. One thing that is most necessary for this production is good DICTION. Gilbert and Sullivan fans will have the original words in their heads, so it is most important that the new words are heard clearly.

As this is a pantomime, as much movement as possible was included: a hornpipe for the King and Servants, a 'passing of the years' ballet (to the music of the Lullaby from 'Cox and Box') between the Christening and Princess Rose's seventeenth birthday, simple routines for the Fairies, and general jubilation for the whole company in the Finale.

I would just like to quote from our press report:

'Easy on the eye, so tuneful to the ear, 'The Sleeping Beauty of Savoy' will deservedly feature in the repertoire of many amateur societies, and could be a winner for smaller professional companies'.

This is a show which the audience will enjoy even if they have never hoard of Gilbert and Sullivan- if they have, they will enjoy it even more. Our company certainly loved doing it, and we were sold out for all twelve performances.' **Jean Bruce.**

John and I hope you'll enjoy reading our Pantomime- those of you who know all Sullivan's tunes so well will be able to have a good 'sing-along'!

Cynthia Morey.

THE SLEEPING BEAUTY OF SAVOY

A Traditional Pantomime

With the Characters of Sir W.S. Gilbert
and the music of Sir Arthur Sullivan

Devised and written
by

Cynthia Morey and John Fryatt

** Please note that Cynthia Morey and John Fryatt hold the copyright of both the <u>Sleeping Beauty of Savoy</u> and <u>Gilbert and Sullivan Gala 2000.</u> On payment of a modest fee, permission to perform these pieces will be readily given. Enquiries to: Crmorey57@aol.com

THE SLEEPING BEAUTY OF SAVOY

This is a traditional Victorian-style Pantomime featuring characters and music from the Gilbert and Sullivan Operas, the latter slightly adapted where necessary, though any alterations are negligible and consist mainly of cuts.

The characters retain the attributes and idiosyncrasies with which Gilbert endowed them, though of course the relationships and situations in which they find themselves are vastly different.

In its construction the Pantomime is similar in shape and length to a typical G & S Opera. There are many allusions, quotations etc which the many thousands of people who are familiar with the Operas would find particularly amusing, though we have tried to refrain from too many 'in' jokes in order to ensure a general appeal.

The 'Sleeping Beauty' theme was chosen because it lends itself so well to the material provided by the Operas. For instance, the scene from *The Sorcerer* in which the villagers fall asleep under the influence of the love potion has an exact parallel in the Pantomime when the Court falls asleep under the influence of the spell. Then Phoebe's spinning song in *The Yeomen of the Guard* at once suggests the song of the Wicked Fairy as she sits at the spinning wheel prior to the pricking of the Princess's finger with the spindle. These are only two examples of apt situations which fit neatly into the pantomime- there are many others.

We felt that by writing the dialogue in rhyming couplets we would be establishing the Victorian flavour of the piece, and also would not appear to be trying to emulate the inimitable dialogue of Sir W S Gilbert.

The star of the show is the Wicked Fairy- 'Mad Meg.' This role should be played by the principal comedian- the type who would normally play the 'Ko-Ko' parts. It is in no way a feminine role, most of the numbers alotted to 'her' being those of the patter variety.

Cynthia Morey and John Fryatt

The Sleeping Beauty of Savoy

Dramatis Personae

KING CORCORAN, A Maritime Monarch   (Baritone)

QUEEN JULIA, (late Julia Jellicoe- Actress)   (Soprano)

PRINCESS ROSE MAYBUD, their Daughter   (Soprano)

EARL TOLLOLLER   ]   (Tenor)
                                      ] Dual Lord Chamberlains
EARL OF MOUNTARARAT]
 (Baritone)

RUTH, the Royal Nursemaid   (Mezzo-Soprano)

THE FAIRY QUEEN, Chief Godmother to the Princess   (Contralto)

CELIA   ]   (Soprano)
LEILA   ]   Professional Fairies, also Godmothers   (Mezzo-
Soprano)
FLETA   ]   (Soprano)

PRINCE HILARION, an Eligible Bachelor   (Tenor)

MAD MEG,   a Wicked Fairy   (Baritone)

CHIEF MINION,   (Baritone)

CHORUS of COURTIERS, LADIES, SERVANTS, MINIONS, FIENDS

ACT I

ACT II

A hundred years elapse between the end of Act I
and the beginning of Act II

ACT I

Scene 1: THE FOREST.

An eerie greenish glow illuminates a fairly dark stage. It comes from a cauldron simmering stage right, stirred by MAD MEG'S Chief MINION. Other MINIONS gather round it.

CHORUS   ('Pour, oh pour the pirate sherry'   The Pirates of Penzance
Act I Opening Chorus)

MINIONS:
Stir, oh stir the cauldron frightful,
Sniff the tantalising smell,
From this recipe delightful
Comes a new and nasty spell!
CHIEF MINION:
Globules ghastly, green and glimmering
Sliding from the slimy spoon-
Keep the cauldron slowly simmering
Till the waning of the moon!

MINIONS:
Watch the cauldron, keep it boiling-
Brewing spells is pleasant toiling!

CHIEF MINION:
Bilious bubbles, rank and reeking
Frolic in the filthy froth,
Soon will victims of our seeking
Taste the black and beastly broth!

MINIONS:
Watch the cauldron, keep it boiling,
Brewing spells is pleasant toiling!
Stir, oh stir etc.

ENTER MAD MEG.

MAD MEG:
Greetings, my minions foul and fell-
Good gracious- what's that gorgeous smell?
(sees cauldron) Aha! Another spell is brewing-
'Twill be the Fairy Queen's undoing!
(sniffs horridly) Delicious- let me have a stir-

CHIEF MINION:
It <u>should</u> be, Ma'am- it's Cauldron Bleu!

MAD MEG (stirs the cauldron with glee, and cackles disgustingly.)
He, he! I'm bad- that's understood-
Yet I do quite a bit of good;
Folk say that venomous am I,
And fiendish too- I can't think why!

SONG: ('If you give me your attention' Princess Ida   Act I)

MAD MEG:

If you give me your attention I will tell you what I am-
(I mean, of course, apart from being mutton dressed as lamb)
In wickedness and witchcraft, willy-nilly I excel,
No naughty necromancer can invent a nasty spell!
In malevolent malpractices I hold a high degree-
I've won at least a hundred silver cups for sorceree;
My experiments in evil always go without a hitch,
Yet everybody says that I am such a wicked witch-
And I can't think why!

My cauldron's always bubbling with a new and nasty spell-
Please drop in for elevenses if you can stand the smell!
I'm a law-abiding citizen as through the air I zoom,
For I hold a current licence for a single-seater broom.

My memory is perfect, not a thing do I forget-
In matters of revenge you'll find I settle every debt;
When weaving webs of wickedness I never drop a stitch,
Yet everybody says that I am such a wicked witch-
And I can't think why!

MINIONS:
She can't think why! She can't think why!

MAD MEG:
Away, my minions, spread your wings-
(And lots of other nasty things)
Around the world in vicious, vile attacks!   (EXIT MINIONS)
I think I'll put me feet up and relax.
And take time off from deepest-dyed deception
To watch my crystal ball (such good reception!)
So, briefly shedding slime and grime and gore,
I'll view- fragrantly refreshed by Chanel 4!

MEG settles herself in her chair in front of her crystal ball. Cross fade
to FAIRY QUEEN and the three FAIRIES in the Fairyvision studio,
grouped round news desk)

QUARTET ('The Soldiers of our Queen' Patience Act I)

FAIRIES:
Appearing on your screen
With news for all the nation
We Fairies-

FAIRY QUEEN:
                    <u>and</u> their Queen!
Are guests upon this station:
Announcing the arrival

Of tiny Princess Royal!
The Monarchy's survived-
So, cheer- each subject loyal!

FAIRIES:
The Monarchy's survived-
So, cheer- each subject loyal!

RECIT: ('Do not give way to this uncalled-for grief' - The Gondoliers-
Act I)

FAIRY QUEEN:
Now we must fly- we're thrilled beyond belief;
This Fairy Newsflash has been very brief.
In later bulletins, a Royal Proclamation
Live coverage will bring- meanwhile, to aviation!
To represent you at the Christening we're invited-
That settled- we trust no other Fairy will feel slighted.

The FAIRIES vanish as MAD MEG furiously switches off the offending
crystal ball.

RECIT: (ctd)
Slighted! No words can be too strong!
Blighted! They <u>all</u> shall be ere long!
Rejected! they'll find an extra guest
Unexpected- to show whose magic's best!
Ha, ha! Ha, ha! Ha, ha!

MAD MEG whirls out in a fury, bound for the Christening. The Forest
fades and the scene changes to the Throne Room.
is revealed.

Scene 2   The THRONE ROOM

SERVANTS and FLUNKEYS are dusting and polishing at breakneck
speed, preparing for the arrival of the Christening GUESTS.

CHORUS: ('Hark, the hour of ten is sounding'   Trial by Jury
Opening Chorus)

Dust the staircase, shake each curtain,
Then make absolutely certain
There is not a speck of dirt in
Any hidden place!
Soon the guests will be converging
On the Palace, seething, surging,
Silk and satin richly merging
With brocade and lace.
Time is short, so we must scurry-
(Parties are an awful worry)
Everybody- hurry, hurry!
Lest we lose our place.
Rub the silver, polish brasses,
Shine the chandelier and glasses,
Goodness me- the time soon passes
At a frenzied pace!

Some SERVANTS collapse, exhausted, on various pieces of furniture,
others fan themselves with dusters etc.

1st FLUNKEY:
Excess of elbow grease and flourished duster
Exhaust me quite (surveys the room) it surely *must* pass muster!

— 15 —

2nd FLUNKEY:
For further news I long, but it's quite plain
Our languid Lords have in their chamber lain-

1st FLUNKEY:
Not so- here comes Mountararat, Tolloller-

2nd FLUNKEY:
(sarcastically) Whe one arrives, the other's sure to foller!

ENTER the two CHAMBERLAINS, LORD TOLLOLLER and LORD MOUNTARARAT

DUET and CHORUS: ('*Two kings of undue pride bereft*' *The Gondoliers Act II*)

SERVANTS:
Two noblemen of bluest blood,
As you, no doubt, can plainly see:
Twin Chamberlains- a role that should
Be one of singularity!
LORDS:
Devoted friends, we made a pact
We'd never part- (and that's a fact)
So now, with King's consent, we act
With absolute equality,
Imbued with tasteful jollity!
SERVANTS:
Two noblemen of bluest blood etc.
LORDS:
With dulcet tones and diction deft
We speak in perfect unity;
Send proclamations right and left
With absolute impunity;

And spread abroad the Monarch's views
In bulletins of daily news,
And promulgate to waiting queues
At every opportunity!
SERVANTS:
Two noblemen of bluest blood etc.

LORD MOUNT: (to LORD TOL)
 True- hearted Thomas!

LORD TOL:
(to LORD MOUNT)　　　　　Generous George!
We'll now momentous news disgorge-

LORD MOUNT:
They're all prodigiously excited-
Let's tell them who the King's invited.

LORD TOL:
(anxiously) No Secrets Act this contravenes?

LORD MOUNT:
(to SERVANTS) Earls, Viscounts, Princes, Kings-

LORD TOL:　　　　　　　　　　　　　-and Queens!

LORD MOUNT:
Tonight will flock into this hall
To join the revels- that's not all-
For, hark to this: across the sky
Four Fairy Godmothers will fly,
Wands and tiaras brightly glistening-
Here to Savoy- just for the Christening!

LORD TOL:
Though offered first class railway fare,
They said they'd rather come by air.

ENTER QUEEN JULIA. She is a very theatrical lady. She glances round at the SERVANTS, who have instantly recommenced a fury of wild dusting.

QUEEN:
Pray stop this energetic dusting
Clean the Crown jewels- (to LORDS) some are rusting!

The CHAMBERLAINS bow assent, dismiss the SERVANTS and hurry off after them.

ENTER RUTH, the Royal Nursemaid.

QUEEN:
Well, how's the Princess this fair morn?
I've had no peace since she was born.
And now her Christening celebration
Means every kind of preparation
Is at this moment under way-
I've come here to escape the fray!

RUTH: (dotingly)
Your Majesty, she grows apace-
Perfect in form as well as face!
I think she'll turn out quite a beauty-
A pity that her Royal duty
Forbids an eminent career,
Or on the stage she might appear!

QUEEN: (theatrically)
My girl, you know not what you say!
Time was when I myself held sway
In every theatre in the land-
The Royal, the Palace and the Grand-
The Opera House, the Hippodrome,
The Globe, the Lyric and the Dome!
Supreme success did I enjoy-
I even played at the Savoy!
Yes, I- your present benefactress
Was- at one time- a famous actress!

RUTH:
(enthralled) Ooh, Madam- tell me all about it!

QUEEN:
I'm going to- how could you doubt it?

DUET ('Long Years ago'   Patience   Act I)

QUEEN:
Some years ago-

RUTH:
(calculating)   Fourteen?

QUEEN:
(crossly)   Maybe!
I was an actress on the stage;
The audience cheered in ecstasy,
And clearly I was all the rage!
Outside the theatre, bearing flowers
My public used to wait for hours,
And gifts arrived from belted earls-

From diamonds down to cultured pearls.
How I adored this great acclaim,
While stealing every scene.
How sweet is fame- yet, all the same-
I'd rather be the Queen!

RUTH:
Oh Madam- what a thrilling life!
But, ere you were a Royal wife-
How <u>did</u> you meet the King?

QUEEN:
Why, he was wearing Naval dress-
I did not know- how could I guess
Such an unlikely thing?

RUTH:
No outward sign of Royalty-
You thought- a humble Captain he-
And wore his diamond ring!

BOTH:
On stage I/you was/were acknowledged Queen;
There's now a simple change of scene
Where I/you, with heart and soul
Still play a leading role!

QUEEN:
I felt I must let down my hair!
Now of my secret <u>you're</u> aware.
Only my husband knew the truth
About the way I spent my youth.
Now that my place is on the throne
The King's not keen to have it known.

RUTH:
Your Majesty, you have my word
I won't repeat what I have heard.
The thought of it gives me the vapours-
How did you keep it from the papers?

QUEEN:
Well- front page news we feared, at least,
Then- suddenly- all printing ccascd-
Papers and magazines alike-
The publishers were all on strike!

ENTER KING CORCORAN. He is an extremely nautical figure in full
dress Naval uniform, plus crown.

RECIT & SONG: ('*My gallant crew- good morning*' *HMS Pinafore
Act I*)

KING:
My gracious wife, good morning!

QUEEN:
Sire- good morning!

KING: (to RUTH)
I trust the babe is well?

RUTH:
Quite well- and you, Sire?

KING:
I am in admirable health, and congratulate my wife once more!

RUTH:
You must feel proud, sire!

SONG: *('I am the Captain of the Pinafore' HMS Pinafore Act I)*

KING:
Of great Savoy I am the Sailor King-

QUEEN & RUTH:
And a salty Sovereign, too!

KING:
Since retiring ashore from the dear old 'Pinafore'
When this landfall came in view!

QUEEN & RUTH:
Since retiring ashore etc.

KING:
They were searching for a King who a little peace would bring
After dire emergencee;
So I tried it for a day, and decided I would stay-
(And it wasn't just the £ s d!)
QUEEN:
His endeavour-

KING: *- was clever!*

RUTH:
He'll stay here-

KING:
                - for ever!
Domiciled in this democracee-
For life is undiluted joy on the smiling sunny shores of old Savoy!

ALL:
For life is undiluted joy etc.

The SERVANTS have entered during this number. They dutifully join in the chorus, dance hornpipe and exeunt.

KING:
Ah, Julia, my dearest wife,
This tiny craft has changed our life!
We're sailing into tranquil water,
Our crew augmented by a daughter.
The throne room's now dressed overall
And decorations fill the hall.
This night will be a great success-

QUEEN:
I really <u>must</u> try on my dress!
(to RUTH) Remember, Nurse- the guests arrive
At, latest, seven-forty-five;
Bring down the Princess sharp at eight-
And, mind- don't be a second late!

RUTH:
(proudly) Princess Rose Maybud, never fear,
Will very punctually appear!

EXEUNT QUEEN and RUTH. KING comes downstage, consulting his watch.

KING:
All should go well, without a doubt.
What <u>are</u> those Chamberlains about?

We find ourselves in a PALACE ANTEROOM for:

Scene 3

ENTER LORD CHAMBERLAINS. They are very weary and harassed.
LORD TOLLOLLER mops his brow.

LORD MOUNT:
Your Majesty, the work is done-
Your orders carried out, each one.

KING:
All influential guests invited?
We don't want any to feel slighted!

LORD MOUNT:
(consulting list) Before we start the feast convivial-
A few more details, Sire- quite trivial-

KING:
(impatiently) Don't bother me with any query,
Opinion, question, doubt or theory-
Initiative you have? Then use it!
More consultation- I refuse it!

TRIO: ('You understand? I think I do'   Ruddigore   Act I)

KING:
You understand?

LORDS: We think we do-

KING:
(severely) I hope you were listening!

LORDS:
You'll find that the Christening
Is nicely planned-

KING:

                                    -and shipshape, too?
With banquet delicious-

LORDS:
You'll find that your wishes
Are carried out with tender care,
From caviare to camembert,
Though fearful the expenses are-

KING:
Don't spoil the ship for a ha'porth of tar!

ALL:
Don't spoil the ship for a ha'porth of tar etc.

EXIT KING

LORD MOUNT:
We've still a list of things to do-

LORD TOL:
Champagne would be very
Much nicer than sherry-

LORD MOUNT:
If you insist-

LORD TOL:
                    It's up to you!
I'll yield to persuasion-

LORD MOUNT:
It's quite an occasion,
The banquet has to be unique-

LORD TOL:
The feast will last at least a week!
Remember what our orders are:

LORD MOUNT:
Don't spoil the ship for a ha'porth of tar!

BOTH:
Don't spoil the ship for a ha'porth of tar etc.

LORD CHAMBERLAINS dance off, arm in arm.

Scene 4   The THRONE ROOM

The scene is one of great elegance. Courtiers and finely-dressed
members of the aristocracy are grouped around the room, awaiting the
arrival of the KING and QUEEN. The Mikado (and suite) and the Duke
and Duchess of Plaza Toro are among them.

*CHORUS: ('With ducal pomp and ducal pride'   The Gondoliers   Act
II)*

MEN:
With pomp and ceremonial pride-

LADIES:
In stately dresses and with well-curled tresses,

ALL:
Gathering here from far and wide on this most joyous day.

MEN:
And to the banquet soon we'll press-

LADIES:
Bring jubilation to this celebration!

ALL:
Our new Princess we come to bless- long life to her today!

ENTER KING and QUEEN

KING:
This reception warm and loyal
Touches King-

QUEEN: -and Consort Royal-
(to lighting desk) May I have a little bit more light?

KING:
Welcome to the banquet here tonight!
Now our future seems a bright one-

QUEEN:
(crossly, as a spot focusses on her) That should be a <u>pink</u> spot, not a white one!
(this is hastily corrected)

KING:
As through life we sail-

QUEEN: (to Lady-in-Waiting) Is my make-up pale?

KING:
In contented state-

QUEEN: (to page) Is my crown on straight?

KING:
I'll retain the helm of this splendid realm!

CHORUS:
Then to the banquet soon we'll press etc.

KING:
The Queen and I, with one accord
Welcome our honoured guests on board,
For at this function, fine and festive-
(aside to QUEEN, who is stifling a yawn) I'll keep it short, dear- don't
get restive!
Tonight- as everybody knows-
We're here to launch the Princess Rose!

All applaud politely. Enter RUTH carrying the baby, and everyone
crowds round in admiration. ENTER LORD CHAMBERLAINS. They
are in a state of great excitement and agitation.

LORD MOUNT:
Your Majesties! Lords, Ladies dear-
The Fairy Godmothers are here!

LORD TOL:
(to orchestra) A fanfare, quick- or roll on drum-

LORD MOUNT:
No time for that, for here they come!

ENTER CELIA, LEILA and FLETA. They smile graciously, and
perform their obviously familiar routine with a practised smoothness
indicative of frequent (and remunerative) repetition.

*TRIO: ('We are dainty little Fairies'   Iolanthe Act I   Opening
Chorus)*

LEILA:
With polite felicitations and in ceremonial raiment
We attend all celebrations (for a very modest payment)

CELIA:
Ever graciously declining all gratuities prodigious;
With our wands discreetly shining we impart an air prestigious!

FLETA:
We impart an air prestigious, most prestigious!

ALL:
Garden parties, fetes and dances- how our presence each enhances,
You can hire us Fairies three for a reasonable fee!

ENTER FAIRY QUEEN

FAIRY QUEEN:
Your mortal Majesties, a greeting!
We <u>have</u> looked forward to this meeting.
I've put aside affairs of State-

(aside) Don't fidget, Fleta, stand up straight !
To mark the Christening of your daughter
Some priceless gift we fays have brought her.
When she receives them, you'll agree
That Princess Rose will surely be
The luckiest child in fact- or fiction!
(aside to FAIRIES) Speak clearly now- and watch your diction!

CELIA:
Wisdom's my gift: you soon shall find
That Rose is Queen of maidenkind.

LEILA:
I give her beauty: Folk will say
That fair is Rose as bright May Day.

FLETA:
Here is my gift- most precious yet:
This hallowed Book of Etiquette!

The FAIRY QUEEN steps forward to present her own gift when
suddenly the stage darkens, there is a flash, and MAD MEG appears.
The FAIRY QUEEN quickly conceals herself.

SCENA: ('Your Revels cease!' The Mikado Act I Finale)

MAD MEG:
Your revels cease! Attention, all of you!

ALL:
A Wicked Fairy hither flies to ruin our festivities!

MAD MEG:
I claim revenge, and retribution too!

Oh, fools, my invitation to forget!

ALL:
Go, leave us all and fly away!

MAD MEG:
I shall remain until I've paid my debt!

ALL:
Away, away! Ill-natured Fay!

FAIRY QUEEN:
(aside, to FAIRIES) Ah, tis Fairy Meg-
The Fay of whom I warned you!

MAD MEG:
(to QUEEN, who kneels in supplication) No! In vain you beg-
For many years I've scorned you!

Oh, fools- forgetting your foremost guest!
You'll soon be fretting at my behest!
For, when your daughter is seventeen-
Ah, then comes slaughter from spindle keen;
A spinning wheel shall seal her fate-
There's no appeal against my hate!
The spindle's dart shall pierce her hand,
She'll play her part as I have planned-
Then, with a mortal cry the Princess Rose shall die!

ALL: (horrified) A spinning wheel shall seal her fate-
There's no appeal against such hate!

MAD MEG gives an ear-splitting cackle of triumph. The GUESTS are
appalled, the QUEEN weeps and the KING tries to comfort her.

KING:
Oh fearful sprite, your wrath withold!
We'll give you rubies- diamonds- gold-
If only you'll retract your threat,
Forgive our rudeness and forget!

QUEEN: (desperately) Great Fairy- hear a mother's prayer:
Spare thou Savoy's defenceless heir!

MAD MEG:
Enough! To late to plead and whine-
The die is cast. Revenge is mine!

Another shrill scream of laughter is cut short as the FAIRY QUEEN
steps forward and reveals herself. MAD MEG visibly recoils.

FAIRY QUEEN:

Foul apparition of the night,
No wonder they did not invite
A beldam so unprepossessing
To give their cherished child her blessing!
I stood aside and slyly waited
Till your black venom had abated.
I have as yet to give my gift-
And though your spell I cannot lift,
I'll use my powers against your hate,
Its full effect to mitigate.
I shall defeat you for the nonce-
So- honi soit qui mal y pense!

The FAIRY QUEEN snaps her fingers contemptuously at MAD MEG

SONG: ('O Foolish Fay'   Iolanthe   Act II)

FAIRY QUEEN:
O foolish Fay, Your evil spite
Has brought dismay this joyous night,
But I've a way to put things right.
(TO QUEEN) Your child won't die- come, dry your tears-
Asleep she'll lie a hundred years,
Untroubled by all worldly fears-
It's not as bad as it appears!
Be of good cheer; I vow we won't forsake her-
We promise this: with loving kiss
A handsome Prince shall wake her!
FAIRIES:
Be of good cheer etc.

MAD MEG cackles scornfully.

MAD MEG:
Your magic powers I must salute!
My spell you've managed to commute
To one of sleep from one of death.
However, I shan't waste my breath
In argument or altercation-
It's just a temporary complication!
I'll bide my time, and intervene
When Princess Rose is seventeen!

She cackles horribly once more, and vanishes in a puff of smoke.

QUEEN:
She's gone! But what profound distress
She's brought to us and the Princess.
What wickedness, what dreadful cunning-

(aside to KING) I'm certain my mascara's running!

She weeps afresh. The KING tries to console her.

KING:
Be comforted, my love. We'll see
If some solution there might be.
(to FAIRY QUEEN) To you, Ma'am, and your Fairies dear
Our gratitude must be made clear.
And also heart-felt thanks included
For intervening then, as you did.
One thing is certain: from this land
All spinning wheels are henceforth banned.
If none exist, all will be well,
For this will nullify the spell.

LORD MOUNT:
(aside to LORD TOL) Oh, Thomas, friend- what sweet relief!
Catastrophe beyond belief
Was nearly caused through our neglect-

LORD TOL:
We should have had the guest list checked!

LORD MOUNT:
Cheer up! the Princess, it appears,
At worst will sleep a hundred years-

LORD TOL:
(thoughtfully) Then be aroused by comely youth-
Not such a dreadful fate, forsooth!

KING:
(heartily) Come now- we've had enough of gloom!

Our celebrations let's resume.
Forget these cares- for now, at least-
Bon appetit! Let's to the feast!

CHORUS   ('Now to the banquet we press'   The Sorcerer   Act I)

ALL:
Now for the banquet divine, now for the pate de foie!
Now for the sparkling wine, now for the caviare!
Now for the turkey supreme, now for the strawberry ice,
Now for the peaches and cream, and now for the chocolate slice!

EXEUNT OMNES, dancing, to the Banquet.

The stage slowly darkens, and a short musical interlude denotes the passing of time. This can also be expressed in the form of a ballet behind a gauze, depicting the Princess's childhood and growing-up years, using children of three ages - ending with the Princess herself, and fading as the FAIRY QUEEN appears in her usual pink spot.

FAIRY QUEEN:
How swift the passing of the years!
Here in Savoy, it now appears
That all is tranquil; Princess Rose
In beauty and in wisdom grows.
For since that fateful Christening feast
All spinning in the land has ceased.
The Wicked Fairy must feel thwarted,
For all their cloth is now imported.
And then, I've been around- a feature
Which probably deters the creature.
I've never any time to spare-
My help is needed everywhere.
And- goodness me, I must away
To Westminster without delay-
I've just remembered that I sent
A young man into Parliament!

EXIT FAIRY QUEEN, in a great hurry.   ENTER MAD MEG, stage left, in a green spot. She gives her usual revolting cackle.

MAD MEG:
Aha! She's gone! She'd no idea
That I was slyly lurking near!
For all these years I've nursed my hate
And waited for a certain date-
It's here at last! My debt I'll pay!
Rose Maybud's seventeen today!

So . . . . spinning wheels have been forbidden?
He, he! I've one discreetly hidden
In far-off turret, dim and shady-
A birthday present for milady!
(Girlish laughter is heard in the distance) Just hearken to that sound repulsive-
It fills me with disgust compulsive!
(She peers offstage) The Princess and her friends draw near-
I'll lure the foolish maidens here,
Then cause her playmates to desert her-
Of course- (cackles) I've no desire to hurt her!

MAD MEG conceals herself.

SCENE 5   A ROOFTOP TERRACE in the PALACE.

ENTER the PRINCESS'S COMPANIONS, searching for her in a game of Hide and Seek.

CHORUS: ('Climbing over rocky mountain' The Pirates of Penzance Act I)

GIRLS:
Climbing over castle stairway,
Ranging far, we've come a fair way,
Hiding, seeking, running hither, thither.
Girlish senses all a-quiver,
(Ancient cobwebs make one shiver!)
In our lofty new domain, our new domain.
Treading dark and stony mazes-
(Spiders giving startled gazes!)
Till before us now the prospect dazes!
Wond'ring where our lost Princess is-
Hoping we've not spoiled our dresses,
Here at last the heights we gain!

They search for the PRINCESS, who suddenly appears in their midst, laughing at their startled surprise.

PRINCESS:
Dear companions of my leisure,
Join me now in youthful pleasure,
Far from stern and watchful eye-
Take the moments as they fly!

GIRLS:
Far from stern and watchful eye-
Greet the moments as they fly!

PRINCESS:
Come, we'll dance a graceful measure,
Birthday joys we all may treasure-
Greet them with a gladsome cry-
Carefree days without a sigh!

GIRLS:
Greet them with a gladsome cry-
Carefree days without a sigh!
Come, we'll dance etc.

PRINCESS:
Our games have led us rather far afield!
Those tiresome Court officials soon will murmur
If we are absent. No, dear friends, we'll yield-
Exchanging terrace top for terra firma!
Go- pave the way for me, and tell my Nurse
I'll come anon to finish my toilette.
Meanwhile- a precious moment quite alone-
Away from protocol and etiquette!

EXEUNT GIRLS.

SONG: ('If somebody there chanced to be' Ruddigore Act I)

PRINCESS:
So now at last I'm seventeen-
Bewild'ring and romantic age!
When thoughts of love must blush unseen
Within my secret diary's page.
Forgotten now are dolls and toys,
My fancies turn to thoughts of- boys!
I dream of boys, a team of boys-
In fact- an endless stream of boys!
Ah . . . .
Escorting me to glitt'ring balls
Where we would dance and pirouette;
Drifting by moonlit terrace walls-
Twin figures framed in silhouette!
But these, of course, are only dreams,
Despised, I'm sure, by etiquette-
(gets out book) Invaluable book!
Now, let me look . . . .
(consults book) Of course! Such conduct brands one a coquette!

My childhood, I need hardly say,
Was sheltered, safe, secure- and dull!
(Though loved, of course, in every way)
I long to live life to the full.
But how can I convince the Court
My Royal favours can't be bought?
I vowed long since
I'd choose my Prince-
Their marriage plans will come to nought!
But with my true love by my side-
A man, and not a marionette,
Those future plans I'd view with pride,

Emblazoned in the Court Gazette!
Though some may find my conduct strange,
And think it just a passing whim-
Until that day
I'll simply say:
Forget your etiquette- and wait for him!

Ah, well- that moment in the future lies-
Meanwhile, my birthday celebrations call.
(looks around her) But, stay- I can't say that I recognise
This section of the palace- not at all.
I'm drawn here by some strange magnetic force-
That strange exotic sound that's just beginning-
I feel I must investigate its source
Although it sends my head and senses spinning!

Cobwebs part to reveal MAD MEG seated at a spinning wheel amist the
shadows.

SONG: ('When maiden loves' The Yeomen of the Guard- Act I)

MAD MEG:
When fiendish Fairy weaves her spell
In twisted turret high,
The damsel, drawn here by my art
Will feel the fatal spindle's dart
Bidding life goodbye!
Blood-curdling banshee yell- aha!
Helps all my spells to jell- aha!
Driven by hate
My wheel of Fate
Will weave a web of wondrous woe!
Doom and distress!
Ill-starred Princess:

Your dream of happiness laid low!
Laid low! Laid low!
This Sorceress
Her wrongs will redress-
Your happiness vanishes at one blow!

The PRINCESS, emerges from her trance-like state and looks around her in a bewildered fashion. Her gaze lights on MAD MEG, who smiles at her ingratiatingly.

DUET: ('Dear friends take pity on my lot' The Sorcerer Act II)

PRINCESS:
What brings me to this curious room?
It is enchantment, surely!
This ancient dame amid the gloom
I'll now approach demurely.
(to MAD MEG) Pray, tell me- I don't wish to pry-
I'd like to know sincerely
The how, the what, the which and why
Of this contraption that you ply-
I'd love to try it, dearly.

MAD MEG:
Come closer here, beside me, dear-
So you may see it clearly!

PRINCESS:
Oh, yes- I'd love to try it, try it dearly!

MAD MEG seizes the PRINCESS and punctures her finger with the spindle. She cries out, and slips lifeless to the floor.

MAD MEG:
(triumphantly) Her finger's pricked, and creeping 'neath her nail is
A poison, deadlier far than *digit*-alis!
A Rose without a thorn- ain't it ironic?
This pinprick brings on slumber catatonic!
Sleep on, my pretty dear, though mountains quake!
Through flood, fire, tempest- you shall never wake!

She cackles in triumph, her mission accomplished.

Scene 6

We are transported to the Throne Room, where the GUESTS are
assembled for PRINCESS ROSE MAYBUD'S birthday party. The
LORD CHAMBERLAINS sadly come forward, lift up the PRINCESS
and carry her to a couch, where they lay her gently. The QUEEN sobs,
the KING tries to comfort her, while the LADIES and GENTLEMEN of
the Court look on in horror.

ENTER FAIRY QUEEN.

FAIRY QUEEN: (to MAD MEG:)
Desist! I'll now defeat your deed disgusting!
How shameful, still for vengeance to be lusting.

Your fall from Fairy grace I find distressing-
Remember what you are, and whom addressing!

INCANTATION ('Every bill and every measure' Iolanthe Act I)

FAIRY QUEEN:
For my power, in ample measure
Serves to cancel your displeasure;
Though your fury it arouses-
I shall guard her while she drowses!

MAD MEG:
Oh!

FAIRY QUEEN:
She shall sleep- I have my reasons-
Through a century of seasons!

MAD MEG:
No!

FAIRY QUEEN:
Drift and dream of pure delights
Through those rather lengthy nights!

MAD MEG:
No, no!

FAIRY QUEEN:
Till some daring Prince has kissed her-
Risking danger to assist her!

MAD MEG:
Aaaah!

FAIRY QUEEN:
Weave around this spot till then
Ferny forest, misty fen.

MAD MEG:
Ohhh!

FAIRY QUEEN:
Cherished now by Fairydom,
King, Queen, subjects of all station,

Sleep shall compass and benumb-
A sort of long-term hibernation!

MAD MEG:
Aaarrrghhh. . . . .!!!

MAD MEG flees, with an ear-splitting cry of anger and frustration, foiled for the time being by the FAIRY QUEEN. the LADIES and GENTLEMEN of the Court stifle yawns as the spell begins to work.

CHORUS: ('Oh marvellous illusion' The Sorcerer Act I)
ALL:
What is this strange delusion
That takes me by surprise,
While comatose confusion
Assails my aching eyes?
Drowsy and quite defenceless,
I cannot struggle more-
Subsiding slowly senseless
Upon the parquet floor!

At the end of this chorus, the entire Court of Savoy is wrapped in deep slumber. The FAIRY QUEEN regards the scene with satisfaction. She raises her wand, the lights slowly fade and the curtain falls.

END OF ACT I

ACT II

Scene 1   The Forest

Everything is wild and overgrown; all that can be seen of the Palace is a glimpse of a turret between the trees. The three FAIRIES are discovered in a clearing. They are quite unmistakably fed up.

TRIO: ('When all night long a chap remains'   Iolanthe Act II)

ALL:
On sentry-go a hundred years!
The duty's not exactly thrilling us-
In fact, we're simply bored to tears,

LEILA:
But- worse than that- our feet are killing us!

CELIA:
We long for London-

LEILA:
> *Paris-*

FLETA:
> *Rome-*

ALL:
Or any of the big metropoli;

LEILA:
Instead, we have to stay at home
And play at Patience or Monopoly!

ALL:
A century! We've missed so much-

CELIA:
Parties and balls-

FLETA:
Seats in the stalls!
We're absolutely out of touch-
Day after dull day-

CELIA:
No operetta to enjoy-
The latest one from the Savoy-

LEILA:
Our willing ears would be beguiled
By witty plays from Oscar Wilde-

CELIA:
(sharply) 'Earnest' or not-
March on the spot! (they obey reluctantly)
For if the Queen should pass this way
She'll clip our wings and dock our pay!
One! Two!!! THREE!!!

The three FAIRIES hastily resume military exercises, albeit rather reluctantly. Their energy is short-lived however, and they soon sink back into lethargy.

FLETA:
A hundred years have swiftly passed,
With Princess Rose still sleeping fast.

CELIA:
I'm sure that we're no longer needed-
The threat of danger has receded,
For Meg, and those of her affinity
No more reside in this vicinity.

LEILA:
Yes- she, no doubt, will all her legions
Has gone to bother other regions.

CELIA:
That's settled! Let's collect our things-

LEILA:
We'll tidy up, then spread our wings!

The three FAIRIES proceed to comb their hair, powder their noses etc.
During this, the FAIRY QUEEN has entered unobserved. She takes in
the whole scene at a glance.

FAIRY QUEEN:
(angrily) Why, what is this, you idle Fays?
You should be spending all your days
Patrolling Palace path and park
In daylight hours, and after dark!
The Prince is due, for goodness' sake
To kiss the Princess Rose awake.
Mad Meg lurks nearby, I suspect,
And all because of your neglect.
Throw out those futile aids to beauty-
Reform your ranks, resume your duty!

The three FAIRIES, crestfallen, hasten to obey.

QUARTET   ('So please you sir, we much regret'   The Mikado Act I)

FAIRIES:
Oh Madam, we apologise-
We fear you took us by surprise
Just trying out some beauty hints
To look our best to greet the Prince!

LEILA: (slyly) that <u>you</u> don't need adornment, too,
You must admit is hard on us-

CELIA:
We're not as beautiful as <u>you</u>-
So sympathise, and pardon us
If we resort to dyes and tints,
Tra la la la la la-

FAIRIES:
That <u>you</u> don't need adornment, too, is hard on us,
We're not as beautiful as <u>you</u>, so pardon us!
Tra la la la la la la la la etc.

FAIRY QUEEN:
I think you ought to recollect
You're guilty of extreme neglect:
Your job, as everybody knows
Is watching over Princess Rose.
Such conduct as I've witnessed here
Impels me to be hard on you,
But as we're short of staff, I fear
I'll simply have to pardon you-
Get back to work at once, d'you hear!

FAIRIES:
Tra la la la la la!

Our conduct here impels her to be hard on us,
But- short of staff- she'll simply have to pardon us!
Tra la la la la la la la la etc.

EXIT FAIRIES, abashed, watched sternly by the FAIRY QUEEN. MAD
MEG creeps in unobserved.

MAD MEG:
He, he! It's good to know what's cooking-
I crept in when she wasn't looking!

The FAIRY QUEEN spins round at the sound of her voice.

FAIRY QUEEN:
Retreat, you grisly apparition!
You should be showing some contrition
Instead of gloating on your malice
Towards the sleepers at the Palace.
Be warned! You've caused enough affray,
And if your deeds in any way
Incur my further disapproval,
I'll engineer your swift removal!

DUET   ('So go to him and say to him' Patience Act II)

FAIRY QUEEN:
For goodness' sake, please undertake to be less base and bestial!

MAD MEG:
I shan't agree, don't lecture me-
Your sermon I'll ignore!

FAIRY QUEEN:
I'll see that you're expelled from our community celestial!

MAD MEG:
If that is so, I'm glad to go-
I find you such a bore!

FAIRY QUEEN:
You'll shed that fearful frown and smile with gentle jocularity,
You'll laugh with Fairy laughter, not that cackle of hilarity,
You'll tear up all your spells and you'll engage in works of charity!

MAD MEG:
I shan't agree, don't lecture me-
Your sermon I'll ignore!
If that is so, I'm glad to go-
I find you such a bore!

Please go away, I shan't obey your orders dictatorial!

FAIRY QUEEN:
A good deed done is much more fun-
Repentance you'd enjoy!

MAD MEG:
I do not wish to hear your sanctimonious tutorial!

FAIRY QUEEN:
Oh, evil Fay, I'll find a way
Your power to destroy!

MAD MEG:
I am the greatest Fairy, with my talent astronomical,
My recipes for poison are concise and economical,
So kindly do not utter threats that I find far from comical!

FAIRY QUEEN:
A good deed done is much more fun-
Repentance you'd enjoy!

MAD MEG:
Oh, virtuous Fay, please go away-
Or evil I'll deploy!

BOTH:
A good deed done is much more fun etc.
Oh, virtuous Fay, please go away etc.

EXIT FAIRY QUEEN

MAD MEG:
I'm glad she's gone! her powers persuasive
Required my tactics most evasive
In order to avoid the sentence
Of retribution and repentance!
Good deeds? Bah! There's no use denying
That vice is much more satisfying!
Who's that? (peers offstage) The prince! A handsome gent!
I wonder if I should repent?
No! better his annihilation-
I'll hide until the confrontation!

EXIT MAD MEG into the FOREST. ENTER PRINCE HILARION. He
is dressed in a simple hunting costume.

SONG: ('Oh, is there not one maiden breast' *The Pirates of
Penzance' Act I)*

PRINCE:
How sweet from Royalty to fly,

Disguised as one of lowly station,
'Neath Nature's canopy to lie,
Enjoying fruits of 'conservation'.
All princely duties laid aside-
Though conscience urges my contrition-
For I, alas, must choose a bride,
A Princess of my own condition.
But how should I decide
Which one to spend my life beside?
Oh, pity my unfortunate position!

If free- like any other boy-
To win and woo my future lady,
Romantic trysts we might enjoy
Within these forest cool and shady.
Then wedded bliss would seal our love-
Devotion duly we'd discover;
And, tender as the turtle dove-
I swear that all my life I'd love her.
If somewhere I might find true love-
For all my life I swear I'd love her!

ENTER FAIRY QUEEN:

FAIRY QUEEN:
Your pardon! I was in yon clearing,
And thus could not help overhearing
Your musical soliloquising.
Prepare yourself for news surprising:
A bride you seek- of Royal birth?
Why, that's the simplest thing on earth!
That is, if valour you possess-
For yonder lies a fair Princess
Condemned to sleep a century since,
Awaiting some intrepid Prince!

PRINCE:
(aside) Ah- 'tis not every day, I ween,
One dallies with a Fairy Queen!
(aloud) A hundred years! I fear she'd be
A century too old for me!

FAIRY QUEEN:
Not so! For time has passed her by;
She does in sweet seclusion lie
Untroubled, carefree and serene,
Just as she was at seventeen.

PRINCE:
Madam, I bless your intervention.
But- how to find the maid you mention?
For all around, where'er one glances,
Thick undergrowth the view enhances.

FAIRY QUEEN:
Through thorny thicket, dark and dense,
You'll pass, ere you find recompense;
Great dangers lurk amid the shade,
But persevere- be not afraid.
The Palace, hid by vines and creepers,
Shelters the loveliest of sleepers;
And when you manage to unearth it,
I rather think you'll find she's worth it!

The FAIRY QUEEN raises her wand; the stage darkens and the
PRINCESS is revealed behind a gauze, asleep on her couch. The
PRINCE is entranced at the sight. The PRINCESS stirs, sits up, and
seeing the PRINCE, stretches out her arms towards him.

DUET: ('None shall part us from each other'   Iolanthe   Act I)

PRINCESS:
Surely destined for each other,
Come, true love, and make us one;
Seek me where the thorn trees smother
Brightness from the kindly sun.

BOTH:
Thou/I the solace of my/thy sleeping,
Thou/I the world wherein I/you dwell,
Thou/I the radiance slowly creeping
Through the darkness of my/thy cell.

PRINCE:
I must hasten to our meeting,
When in joy you'll wake to find
That the hundred years seem fleeting,
And the cruel spell seems kind.

BOTH:
Thou/I the answer to my pleading,
Thine/mine the power this spell to break,
Thine/mine the path toward me/thee leading,
At thy/my kisses I'll/you'll awake!

The PRINCE moves towards the PRINCESS, arms outstretched. She tries in vain to reach him, but the lights fade and she is gone.

PRINCE:
Stay, shadowy captor of my heart!
I curse the sorcerer's magic art
Which binds thee thus with brutal spell-
(turns to FAIRY QUEEN) Dear Madam- Oh! She's gone as well!

My mind's made up. Though snares be laid
Within the deadly forest's shade,
I'll brave whatever may transpire
To gain at last my heart's desire!

As the PRINCE prepares to enter the Forest, the stage darkens and
MAD MEG glides on to confront him. She calls her FIENDISH
FOLLOWERS.

INCANTATION: ('Sprites of earth and air'   The Sorcerer   Act I)

MAD MEG:
Foulest fiends of night-
Gibbering ghouls that glower:
Seethe and swarm in spectral storm
To prove the potion's power!
Draw near! Draw near! Draw near!

FIENDS:
(off stage) Mad mistress, we are here!

MAD MEG:
Demons, dread and dire-
Hellish hounds that bay-
Leprous things with leathery wings
Now bar the Prince's way!
Draw near! Draw near! Draw near!

FIENDS:
Mad mistress, we'll appear!

ENTER FIENDS, in various evil forms.

PRINCE:
(horrified) See, see- they assemble-
Dread creatures of night!

ENTER FAIRY QUEEN and FAIRIES

FAIRY QUEEN:
'Tis no time to dissemble-
Prepare now to fight!

The FAIRY QUEEN hands the PRINCE a Magic Sword

MAD MEG:
'Mid sulphorous reek, with searing shriek
Bring bilious magic black!
Dread demons dire 'mid flickering fire
Fly forth in wild attack!
Come, creatures coarse in gathering force
With tearing talons mince!
And gargoyles grim tear limb from limb
This brash intruding Prince!
(summons more FIENDS)   Fiends in force!

FIENDS:
Here, of course!

MAD MEG:
Demons black!

ENTER more FIENDS, even more terrible.

FIENDS:
We'll attack!

MAD MEG: (wildly) TO THE KILL !!

MUSIC continues as deadly fight ensues, and the PRINCE finally
succeeds in vanquishing MAD MEG with the aid of the MAGIC
SWORD. MAD MEG and her FIENDS retreat. The PRINCE enters
the Forest, and the scene dissolves into the THRONE ROOM at the
PALACE, where the PRINCESS slumbers peacefully on her couch.
The COURT are still fast asleep in the attitudes they assumed a century
ago. Everything and everybody is covered with cobwebs. ENTER the
PRINCE. He looks around in wonder at the strange scene, then sees the
PRINCESS. He is entranced.

DUET:　　　*('Were you not to Ko-Ko plighted'　The Mikado　Act I)*

PRINCE:
Fairest form I see before me,
Stirring love within my breast!
Oh, how easy to adore thee-
You're the ending of my quest.
Just one moment's hesitation
Lost in wonder, lost in bliss,
Then Love's purest consummation:
I'll awake thee with a kiss!　(he does so)

BOTH:
I'll/he'll awake thee/me with a kiss.

PRINCESS:
(gazing at him in rapture) Goodness me- a manly torso!
Like my dreams were, only more so!
Have the kindly Fates above me
Sent this Prince and does he love me?

PRINCE:
Loves you etc

PRINCESS:
Loves me etc

PRINCE:
Thus in love's capitulation
Happy girl and happy boy
Melt in mutual admiration,
Henceforth love shall be without alloy-
Life will be unending joy!
Let me make it clear to you
This is what we'll <u>always</u> do! (he kisses her again)

BOTH:
Kiss, and kiss, and kiss, and kiss-
This is what we'll <u>always</u> do!

EXEUNT PRINCE and PRINCESS ecstatically.

Now all around the THRONE ROOM people are beginning to stir, as the spell loses its power. The KING, on the verge of waking, has obviously been dreaming of his nautical days.

KING:
Avast! Belay! All hands on deck!
Reef in the topsail- Ouch! My neck!
I've dreadful cramp from head to toes-
This throne's a poor place for a doze!
(he looks round dazedly) This stateroom's looking far from stately-
Those stewards can't have dusted lately!
(yawns) I must have dropped right off- hey, sirrah-
(digs Mountararat in the ribs) What time is it?

QUEEN: (waking with a start)   Here, quick- my mirror!

LORD MOUNT:
My watch has stopped- or else it's slow-
'Twas wound a hundred years ago-

LORD TOL:
Good heavens, yes- a century's passed-
However did it go so fast?
I've not the slightest recollection-

QUEEN:
(gloomily into mirror) It's not done much for my complexion!

LORD TOL: (to LORD MOUNT) You've gone quite grey- I also must-

LORD MOUNT:
You idiot! It's only dust-
(brushes it off) Your hair's still brown-

LORD TOL:

                              Oh, what a boon-
I didn't want to dye so soon!

QUEEN:
(alarmed) Where's Princess Rose? The door's ajar-

RUTH:
(soothingly) Her bed's still warm- she's not gone far.

ENTER PRINCE and PRINCESS

PRINCESS:
Why, Mother- Father- <u>all</u> awake?
I stepped outside, some air to take.
And, free from soporific spell,
I fear I took this *heir* as well!
(The heir to an illustrious throne-
So my bold conduct please condone!)
'Tis Prince Hilarion the brave,
Who fought his way, my life to save,
Through dangers devilishly planned-

PRINCE:
I beg to claim your daughter's hand!

KING: (delighted) My boy- there's nothing we'd like better-
'Twas good of you to come and get her!

QUEEN:
Your offer we will gladly take up!
That's settled, then- now, where's my make-up?

KING:
Lords, ladies, everyone- make haste-
The wedding feast- no time to waste!

With a buzz of excitement the LADIES and GENTLEMEN of the Court
bow and EXEUNT.

QUARTET: ('Then one of us will be a Queen'   The Gondoliers
Act I)

PRINCESS:
I was quite aghast that a century passed
Since I took to my Royal bed;

I could make a list of the things I have missed
And the words that have not been said.
Till a passionate kiss of a Princely kind
Took me suddenly by surprise;
I can't agree that Love is blind-
It's opened <u>both</u> my eyes!

ALL:
Oh-
'Tis a curious thing, this counting sheep
Through a hundred years of sleep-
While soundly locked in slumber deep
Through a century of sleep!

PRINCE:
I little thought at my father's Court
What the future had in store,
As some new Princess from a good address
Would chatter and bleat and bore!
But the beauty I've found has wit and charm
Plus a character warm and gay;
I wakened her without 'alarm'
And she 'rose' to greet the day!

ALL:
Oh-
'Tis a curious thing etc.

QUEEN:
When I heard, my dears, that a hundred years
Had suddenly slipped away,
I was quite dismayed till my glass displayed
That I hadn't aged a day!
So, fresh and fragrant once again

My spirits have gaily soared;
In Queenly dignity I'll reign-
I'm 'regally restored'!

ALL:
Oh-
'Tis a curious thing etc.

KING:
The briefest nap for a Naval chap
Is the most he expects of sleep;
So I felt most shocked to be soundly rocked
In the cradle of the deep!
But now that I've surfaced once again
On a swiftly-flowing tide,
In my own wardroom I shall toast the groom
And prepare to 'cast off' the bride!

ALL:
Oh-'Tis a curious thing etc'

At the end of the QUARTET they all dance off to prepare for the Wedding, and we find ourselves in:

Scene 7   The Forest

ENTER MAD MEG, fuming.

MAD MEG:
They've foiled my plots and plans abundant,
And Good's prevailed- so I'm redundant.
I'll sell my spells and with the riches
Endow a home for worn-out witches.

ENTER FAIRY QUEEN

FAIRY QUEEN:
Fie! What unseemly indignation!
Now is your chance for reformation;
With my benevolent assistance
You'll soon live down your past existence.

MAD MEG:
I <u>like</u> being Evil- Good's much duller-
In any case- white's <u>not</u> my colour!

FAIRY QUEEN:
Dont fret- a life of circumspection
Works wonders for a poor complexion;
Soon <u>yours</u> will be no longer sallow,
But pink and shining- like marshmallow!

MAD MEG:
Your kindness fills me with revulsion-
All right! I'll do it- on compulsion!

ENTER CELIA, LEILA, and FLETA, carrying a Fairy dress (which
has obviously seen better days), a crown and a wand for the new Good
FAIRY MEG, who regards them with disgust.

QUARTET: ('There is beauty in the bellow of the blast'   The Mikado
Act II)

FAIRY QUEEN:
Come and join us, spreading virtue through the cast!

MAD MEG:
I prefer it, being quite beyond the pale!

FAIRY QUEEN:
In a gauzy dress alluring, your ill temper we'll be curing-

MAD MEG:
(scowling at dress) And I bet it's one you picked up in a sale!

CELIA:
We admit it's off the peg, dear-

LEILA:
But at least you'll show a leg, dear-

FAIRY QUEEN:
And it's <u>not</u> one that we picked up in a sale!

MAD MEG:
Don't you think that style is frightfully passé?

FAIRY QUEEN: (firmly) It's a classic line that simply never fails!

MAD MEG: Well, it fills me with amazement-
Just direct me to the basement,
I'll select a better bargain from the rails!

CELIA:
If you think that it's a mess, dear-

LEILA:
Go and try at M&S, dear-

QUEEN:
You'll not find a better bargain on the rails!

MAD MEG:
To me it seems a total failure,
This Fairy regalia compulsoree-

FAIRY QUEEN:
Don't fret- you'll soon be gaily submitting,
And happily flitting from tree to tree!

FAIRIES:
To her it seems a total failure etc.

MAD MEG tries to escape her fate, but is pursued by the FAIRIES, bearing her dress and accessories. The FAIRY QUEEN raises her wand, the Forest vanishes, and we find ourselves back in the THRONE ROOM.

Scene 8   The THRONE ROOM

Everything is restored to its original splendour, and richly decorated for the Royal Wedding. Enter LADIES and GENTLEMEN of the Court, magnificently dressed. When they are assembled, ENTER LORD MOUNTARARAT and LORD TOLLOLLER.

DUET and CHORUS: ('Soon as we may, off and away'   Iolanthe   Act II Finale)

LORD MOUNT:
Back at our post,
Ready to toast
Rapturous couple here united.

LORD TOL:
Now from our list
Nobody's missed-
Everyone has been invited!

ALL:
Every, every, every,
Ev'ry one has been invited!

LORDS MOUNT and TOLL:
Though a mistake we made before,
Ponder it well ere you deplore-
Out of disaster came success:
Marriage of Prince to fair Princess!

ALL:
Though a mistake they made before etc.

ENTER KING and QUEEN.   Segue into:

DUET: ('Here's a how-de-do'   The Mikado   Act II)

KING:
In our Royal view
Prince and Princess true
Very soon should rule our nation,
We'll announce our abdication-
Move to pastures new,
Sail the ocean blue-

QUEEN:
Like old times for you!

KING;
Back and forth we'll tack,
Soon acquire the knack!

QUEEN:
Gambling in some far Casino-
Finest food and stacks of vino!
Nothing shall we lack-

BOTH:
Shall we e'er come back?

Even Queens and Kings
Need to spread their wings;

KING:
State occasions- we deplore 'em-

QUEEN:
Quick vacations- we're all for 'em-
Time to pack our things,

BOTH:
Take what pleasure brings,
Fling our final flings!

With some quite amusing cruising
Round the smaller isles of Greece,
Where the bathing is amazing
And the parties never cease!

KING:
We'll take the Royal yacht-

QUEEN:
It's not been used a lot!

BOTH:
Here's a blissful state of things,
A holiday for me and you:
A second honeymoon that's really rather overdue!

KING:
Rather over-

QUEEN:
             Rather over-

KING: *Rather overdue!*

BOTH:
Second honeymoon that's really rather, rather overdue-
Yes, it's rather, rather overdue-
Just for me- and you!

ENTER PRINCE and PRINCESS.   Segue into:

DUET: ('Never mind the why and wherefore'   HMS Pinafore   Act II)

BOTH:
We declare we're both delighted
That our vows are truly plighted,

PRINCESS:
We're a Princess and a Prince of quite abnormal pedigree,

PRINCE:
Though our meeting was 'unconsciously' informal, you'll agree!

BOTH:
Spread the news throughout the nation,
Future days are all set fair-
Celebrate with invitation:
Come and toast the happy pair!

PRINCE:
Through the forest glades he sought her
And from evil clutches caught her-

PRINCESS:
Now a newly-wakened daughter
Earns the happiness he brought her!

BOTH:
Let the air with joy be laden,

ALL:
Spread the news throughout Savoy!

BOTH:
Lucky lad and merry maiden,

ALL:
Happiness for girl and boy!
Farewell, balcony and stalls
As the final curtain falls,
(to PRINCE and PRINCESS)May you both succeed in all you do-
Good fortune prosper you!

General rejoicing, as the FAIRY QUEEN ENTERS to bless the happy couple, accompanied by MAD MEG, who is obliged to join in the celebrations by the three FAIRIES.

THE   END

C U R T A I N

GILBERT AND SULLIVAN GALA 2000

Some random thoughts on this Gala Night

What *is* this D'Oyly Carte thing? Whenever a reunion, concert or gathering of ex-members is suggested, the old grapevine works overtime. 'Where is it?' 'When is it?' 'Who do we get in touch with?' These enquiries keep the phone lines red hot as everyone determines to be part of the projected event.

It'sa strange phenomenon. So many singers from the old D'Oyly Carte went on to sing in grand opera- the old Sadler's Wells (later to become English National Opera) Covent Garden, Glyndebourne, and numerous opera houses throughout Europe. Others turned their attention to musicals and appeared in many West End shows. Some gave up the business altogether, for various reasons. And a few remained with the D'Oyly Carte, to become well-known and much loved favourites with that unique company.

More years than I care to remember have rolled by since most of us were members of that select band, and we are puzzled by the strange magnetism it still holds for us. Sadly- but inevitably- we grow fewer in number. It is wonderful to see the Gilbert and Sullivan heritage being passed on to younger performers, for in their hands lies the future of these timeless operas.

AN UNFORGETTABLE OCCASION

In 1956 I went to Golders Green Hippodrome to see the D'Oyly Carte Opera Company for the very first time. The opera was *Ruddigore* and Rose Maybud was portrayed by a dainty young lady who oozed charm and charisma- it was, of course, Cynthia Morey. I quickly followed this first visit with another. There- in *Trial by Jury*- was John Fryatt- a dashing young tenor who later became an international performer. I could not have imagined that many years later I would be organising a Gilbert and Sullivan charity Gala, and that Cynthia, John, and many others from the D'Oyly Carte would be appearing in it.

It was more than forty years later that I planned a D'Oyly Carte reunion of former members of the Company, together with other other Gilbert and Sullivan artists, at Oak Hall, Sheffield Park, in East Sussex. The occasion was like a huge family gathering, and they all made me feel part of that family. I considered myself very privileged (and rather greedy!) having all these wonderful G & S performers all to myself, and vowed that if there was another opportunity I would try and share my good fortune with others. This is exactly what I did to celebrate the Millennium.

The 2000 Millennium Reunion was to be a two-day event; the reunion on the Saturday, followed by a Gala Charity Concert on the Sunday evening at the Hawth Theatre, Crawley. All the artists agreed to give their services for the benefit of the charity, which was to be the Children's Hospital, Great Ormond Street, and these included former D'Oyly Carte conductors David Steadman and David Mackie. A full professional orchestra had been engaged, and David Steadman had arranged a unique overture which cleverly linked music from all the Savoy Operas. The concert, which depicted all the ups and downs of Gilbert and Sullivan's relationship was to be narrated by Cynthia Morey as the Good Fairy Harmony, and John Fryatt as Demon Discord. For this Cynthia, aided and abetted (as so often!) by John, had written the most wonderful script. Actors Charles Pemberton, Anthony Herrick and Michael Simkins were to play Gilbert, Sullivan and Richard D'Oyly Carte respectively.

Some of the special guests in the audience would include former D'Oyly Carte sopranos Valerie Masterson, Helen Roberts and Joyce Perry (at that time the oldest surviving member of the Company). To give civic support, the Mayor would attend, and Paul Follows, director of Grim's Dyke, Gilbert's former home, had kindly agreed to host these important guests for me.

Cynthia, with the assistance of Alan Spencer, was to direct the entire production. With the brilliant script, and all the wonderful people who were participating, it seemed that we were off to a very good start.

But how were the bookings progressing? I had hired a theatre with almost 1000 seats to fill! Bookings seemed to be very slow coming in, and I could see myself being left with a huge financial bill. Then- all of a sudden- we were fully booked- and turning people away!

The evening proved to be a sensational success, especially when the much-loved tenor Thomas Round (then in his late eighties) danced the hornpipe from *Ruddigore*. The audience were ecstatic- you could hardly hear the orchestra, due to cheering and applause. Another highlight was the moving rendition of 'Alone and yet alive' from *The Mikado*, by Helen Landis, which nearly stopped the show. It was certainly a most memorable evening, and raised a huge donation for Great Ormond Street.

With permission from Cynthia Morey and John Fryatt, who hold the copyright, this wonderful script is now available for everyone to use. It is equally suitable for a large or small cast- so have fun, and enjoy it as much as we did!

Melvyn Tarran
Oak Hall
Sheffield Park East Sussex

GILBERT AND SULLIVAN
GALA 2000

PRESENTED BY MELVYN TARRAN

at
The Hawth Theatre, Crawley
June 25th 2000

Devised by CYNTHIA MOREY
Aided and abetted by JOHN FRYATT

with many former stars of the Savoy Operas

and

THE SAVOY CONCERT ORCHESTRA

Musical Director DAVID STEADMAN
Guest Conductor   DAVID MACKIE

Preceded by a fully-staged production of 'TRIAL BY JURY'
To celebrate its 125th Anniversary

OVERTURE 'SAVOY POT-POURRI'
David Steadman

PLAYLET: HOW 'TRIAL BY JURY' WAS BORN

GAUZE in. Acting area stage right lit. Desk,chair, files papers. It is Richard D'Oyly Carte's office at the Royalty Theatre. He is seated in a rather depressed attitude, going through some papers (box office receipts?) There is a poster advertising 'La Perichole' on the wall. Distant sounds of the operetta can be heard- a performance is in progress.

ENTER GILBERT (possibly from front of house. He crosses to D'Oyly Carte's office)

GILBERT:
Are you there, Mr Carte?

CARTE:
Come in! Oh, it's you, Gilbert.

GILBERT: (entering and peering at papers on desk)
You seem rather worried. Box office takings disappointing?

CARTE: (hastily shuffling papers away from GILBERT'S gaze)
No, it's not that exactly, the audiences like *La Perichole* well enough-
but it's just not long enough. We need a short piece to follow it. *You*
don't have any ideas, I suppose?

GILBERT: (producing a script from his pocket)
Funny you should say that . . . . . (he hands it to CARTE)

CARTE:
What's this? (reads title) *Trial by Jury*- a legal piece?

GILBERT:
Yes- it's a breach of promise case-

CARTE:
Sounds a bit serious for the Royalty-

GILBERT:
Not the way *I've* written it!

CARTE:
Well . . . . take it along to Arthur Sullivan and see what *he* thinks. Ask him if he'll do the music, then we'll have another look at it . . . . .

Lights fade on Carte's office and come up on Sullivan's study left. Follow spot on Gilbert as he crosses stage.
Sullivan is seated at his desk in the throes of composition. There is manuscript paper evrywhere. A decanter of brandy and a glass are to hand.

GILBERT:
Are you there, Sullivan? May I come in?

SULLIVAN: (humming and scribbling furiously)
Who is it? Ah, Gilbert- yes, come in. Just a moment- (he completes a bar) Yes . . . . I think that'll do it- (looks up from his work) This is an unexpected pleasure- what can I do for you?

GILBERT:
Carte wants a short piece to follow *La Perichole* at the Royalty.

SULLIVAN:
Does he, now?

GILBERT:
Well, I happen to have this libretto- it needs setting to music. Would you consider . . . . . Oh, but you may not like it-

SULLIVAN:
I'm rather busy just now- I'm not sure I'll have the time- (GILBERT turns to go) But, wait, old chap- why don't you read it to me, and we'll see?

Trial by Jury music begins, very quietly as GILBERT starts to read. The lights fade gradually, as does his voice, then come up as he finishes the final words ' was affected by a job- and a good job too' SULLIVAN, unnoticed by GILBERT, is convulsed with mirth. GILBERT, sure that his work is a failure, slams his book shut and turns to leave. SULLIVAN bursts out laughing, holding his sides.

GILBERT: (disbelieving) You found it amusing?

SULLIVAN:
It's an absolute gem! It's excellent! I shall love setting it. (he hums 'Oh joy unbounded', beating time as he does so) Leave it with me, Gilbert, old chap- I'll have it done in no time. (they shake hands)

Quick fade on the two men. Slow bleed through gauze on to opening picture of 'Trial' with CHORUS frozen in appropriate attitudes. They come to life with the music, and the action commences:

TRIAL BY JURY

At the end of the opera, on applause, GILBERT and SULLIVAN enter and take their calls.

GILBERT:
Well, how about that, Sullivan!

SULLIVAN;
I must say, they seemed to like it.

GILBERT:
Yes- I think we have a success on our hands. Maybe we'll work together again some time-

SULLIVAN:
Yes, Gilbert- maybe we will!

They shake hands. As their hands touch, the whole stage freezes. Richard D'Oyly Carte enters downstage right. He is rubbing his hands with glee.

CARTE:
If *I* have anything to do with it, they <u>certainly</u> will!

At this, the whole stage comes to life again. There is much noise and merriment, underscored by a reprise of the music of the last chorus of 'Trial'. CARTE crosses centre to congratulate the two men. The house tabs come in on the last 13 bars.

INTERVAL

GILBERT AND SULLIVAN GALA 2000 CONCERT

This is no ordinary concert! It is compered by two characters representing the ups and downs of Gilbert and Sullivan's reign over the world of comic opera. The Good Fairy Harmony is only interested in the promotion and success of the operas, having in mind the pleasure they will bring to so many people who in 1871 were uninitiated in this kind of entertainment. But the evil Demon Discord is bent on disrupting it all. He devises the pitfalls which occur along the way and does his best to ensure the failure of these operas. A struggle ensues- but who wins? I think we all know the answer.

PART II

The stage is dark and set for the concert. Music from *The Mikado* begins. ENTER FAIRY HARMONY from stage right in pink follow spot. Music rapidly changes to *Iolanthe* fairy music. She looks down, annoyed, and hisses at conductor: 'Do you mind? I'm not *that* kind if fairy!' Music quickly dies away. She sees audience, and smiles ingatiatingly.

FAIRY H:
'What's *she* doing here?' I hear you say-
I'll tell you- briefly- if I may,
Explain exactly who I am,
(Apart from mutton dressed as lamb)
My job is flying round the earth
To check up on supplies of mirth;
That's not as dull as it appears-
(Well, I've been doing it for years)
Despite- and this I have to mention-
The Demon Discord's intervention.
I found- in eighteen-seventy-one-
This country didn't have much fun,
With entertainments very few
That one could take the family to.
Something was needed, quite delectable-
Of course, it had to be respectable,
So's not to offend the eyes and ears
Of genteel maids of tender years.
So . . . what to do? Laughter's essential.
I found two chaps of great potential:
A dramatist- of wit satirical,
A young composer, suave and lyrical.

Gilbert and Sullivan the name.
Since then- well, nothing's been the same!
I waved my wand- the two men met-

*There is a terrible discord from the orchestra. DEMON DISCORD
enters stage left in a green follow spot.*

DEMON D:
They did! And then what did we get?
Ah- *Thespis*- or *The Gods Grown Old*-
It's disappeared for good, I'm told-

FAIRY H:
(to audience) This Demon Discord pains me sorely-

DEMON D:
I love being creepy here in Crawley!*   * *(This couplet applies only
to the Hawth production!)*

FAIRY H:
Thespis destroyed? Well, there you're wrong-
We've script, a chorus, and one song-

DEMON D:
One song! What may the title be?

FAIRY H:
Why- 'Little Maid of Arcadee'!

** *Follow spots out, stage to full- this happens before each musical
interlude*

THESPIS
SONG: *Little Maid of Arcadee*

DEMON D:
A sickly, sentimental number-
In me, it just induces slumber. (yawns)

FAIRY H:
(to audience) His attitude fills me with fury.
But what came after? *Trial by Jury!*

TRIAL BY JURY
Selected numbers

DEMON D:
My verdict is- it's far too short-
and *what* a setting- in a court!
No magic there- you call this art?

FAIRY H:
I left the rest to D'Oyly carte.
(When two such elements exist,
They sometimes need a catalyst)
No point in trying to defy you-
This 'Sorcery' may satisfy you.

THE SORCERER
Selected numbers

DEMON D:
A minor triumph, quickly past.
Such trifles very seldom last.
Their mediocre talents plural
Sink without trace mid settings rural.

FAIRY H:
Far from it! Very much afloat,
They've launched a most successful boat-
Just wait until you hear the score
Of witty, sparkling *Pinafore*.

DEMON D:
We'll *have* to have it! So, no more ado-
(to conductor) Maestro, on deck! Conduct your motley crew! (rude
noise from pit) *(EXIT both)*

HMS PINAFORE
Selected numbers

This time, green follow spot stage left only (ENTER DEMON D)

DEMON D:
This great acclaim's beyond a joke.
I, in their wheel, must place a spoke!
It seems the next piece is piratical-
Methinks I'll take a short sabbatical
And sneak these tunes, soon as I may,
To 'pirates' in the USA.
Then frightful versions of the show
Will deal the work a deadly blow!

ENTER Fairy H, follow spot immediately stage right

FAIRY H:
Pirates- in spite of all your talk,
Plays already in New York;
For Richard D'Oyly Carte, it seems,
Is up to all your wicked schemes.
He's filling theatres every night,

Establishing the copyright.
Your plot is foiled ere you employ it-
Why not just sit back and enjoy it?

THE PIRATES OF PENZANCE
Selected numbers

As stage darkens, follow spots stage left only (ENTER DEMON D)

DEMON D:
I sense a flop! Their next brainchild
Is ridiculing Oscar Wilde.
A minor writer, it appears-
His work won't last for many years.
And thus their plot will soon be dated-
A fact they've not anticipated!

Follow spot immediately stage right, retain spot stage left (ENTER FAIRY H)

FAIRY H:
The newest opera, just presented,
Is *Patience*- drawing crowds demented!
The present theatre's far too small,
It can't accommodate them all.
A larger venue now is needed-
A fact that D'Oyly Carte has heeded.
I can announce with pride and joy:
Patience transfers to the Savoy!
Oh- one more thing- that theatre bright
Is lit by new electric light!   *(EXIT BOTH)*

PATIENCE
Selected numbers

Follow spot stage right only. (ENTER FAIRY H)

FAIRY H:
(rather wearily) There's quite a lot of strain and stress
In helping to promote success.
You know- I've really put my heart in it-
They ought to recognise *my* part in it.
I'll put my feet up for a day
And let them go their own sweet way.
They might acknowledge *my* assistance
By recognising my existence! *(EXIT)*

IOLANTHE
Selected numbers

Follow spot stage right only (ENTER FAIRY H)

FAIRY H:
Well, that was nice! They had the sense
To recognise *my* influence!
Their competence they've truly shown-
I think they'll manage on their own
While I attend to other things
Around the globe- thank God for wings! *(EXIT FAIRY H; ENTER DEMON D)*

DEMON D:
She's gone! That gives me greater scope
To interfere in things, I hope.
Already I have stirred the pot:
One's discontented with his lot-
That's Sullivan. He thinks it properer
To start composing grander opera!
He's tired of topsy-turvy schemes-

Of serious work he fondly dreams.
So Gilbert's given in, and tried a
Classic epic- PRINCESS IDA!
What joy- it couldn't be much worse-
Three acts- and written in blank verse!

PRINCESS IDA
Selected numbers

Follow spot stage right only (ENTER FAIRY H)

FAIRY H:
(crossly) I'm only absent for a day,
But what occurs when I'm away
Is most annoying! Trying to do
An opera in format new
Did not quite work. I could have told them.
But never mind- no use to scold them.
A new idea? I've looked around,
But so far no solution found.
But, wait . . . in Knightsbridge all one sees
Are oriental oddities.
They're topical, you must agree-
But how to influence WSG?
A Japanese sword hangs on his wall . . .
I'll wave my wand- that sword shall fall!   *(EXIT FAIRY H)*

THE MIKADO
Selected numbers

Both follow spots on (ENTER FAIRY H AND DEMON D)

FAIRY H:
Well- follow *that!* A mammoth task.
For greater praise you couldn't ask.

DEMON D:
Now Gilbert's plans are all turned down
By Sullivan's disdainful frown.

FAIRY H:
Perhaps a melodrama might
Have possibilities? 'All right,'
Said Sullivan, 'I'll write the score.'
Hence the next opera: RUDDIGORE.

DEMON D:
The audience will jeer and scoff-
The name's enough to put you off!

RUDDIGORE
Selected numbers

DEMON D:
(gleefully) I told you so! The Daily News
featured the headline: 'Audience boos!'

FAIRY H:
The first performance, yes, was stressful-
In later years it was successful,
And quite a favourite, I've heard tell-
(I know the opera rather well!)

DEMON D:
I hired a gallery desperado
To bellow out, 'Bring back Mikado'!
On their careers I'll cast a blight,
And soon they will be finished, quite.
I'll goad old Gilbert, till he's reckoned
Tunes take first place- his words come second!

I'll whisper into Sullivan's ear
That he must scorn each new idea-
Stir up the fragile situation
And hope it ends in litigation!

FAIRY H:
(firmly) It won't! Not yet- for Gilbert's found
A subject that he can expound
Into a story. Long he sought
Real characters, real plot, real thought.
And triumphed, after working hard:
The show? THE YEOMEN OF THE GUARD.

THE YEOMEN OF THE GUARD
Selected numbers

Follow spot stage left only. ENTER DEMON D

DEMON D:
I'm in a 'towering' rage, and time is short-
They've really done much better than I thought.
(considers) Sir Arthur's illness, Gilbert's painful gout-
What better time for this than falling out?

Add follow spot stage right. ENTER FAIRY H

FAIRY H:
Now, hold your tongue! There's yet to be
Another brilliant fantasy;
We're going overseas this time
To love and laugh in sunnier clime,
With wine and roses, smiles and tears
And sumptuous tunes: THE GONDOLIERS!

THE GONDOLIERS
Selected numbers

Follow spot stage left only. ENTER DEMON D

DEMON D:
I'd given up- than I found out
There was an argument about
A carpet laid at the Savoy,
The cost of which did much annoy
Our Gilbert, for he did not see
Why such a liability
Should fall to his account, and thus
He raised objections, made a fuss,
And ultimately went to court
To claim his rights. I felt I ought
To stimulate the argument,
And this I did. in the event
I finally split up the trio,
And sang a victory song, con brio!

Add follow spot stage right. ENTER FAIRY H

FAIRY H:
Stop that ! I'll have you know, my friend-
You haven't won! It's *not* the end.
The three men, at a later date
Decided to collaborate
On quite a moderate success:
UTOPIA LIMITED- no less.

UTOPIA LIMITED
Selected numbers

Both follow spots on. ENTER BOTH

DEMON D:
(exasperated) Have you quite finished? I've fulfilled my task-

FAIRY H:
Oh, no, you haven't- Listen- since you ask-
One more, and only one is left,
And then, indeed, we'll be bereft
Of any further G and S-
But what a saga of success!
So, let this put an end to all your tricks-
THE GRAND DUKE opens: eighteen-ninety-six!

THE GRAND DUKE
Selected numbers

Both follow spot on. ENTER BOTH

DEMON D:
(still fighting) Each ghastly new production proves my case!
Ill-served, these works will vanish without trace-

FAIRY H:
If that is so, then tell me, pray-
(includes audience) What are *we* doing here today?
No G and S? Don't be absurd!
Their very name's a household word.
And new ideas are often fine-
It's knowing *where* to draw the line.
Productions needn't be bizarre-

DEMON D:
As very many of them *are-*
With foolish costumes, business frantic,
And many a pseudo-comic antic,
And altered words, and useless caper-

FAIRY H:
(producing a libretto) Read what *they* say- it's down on paper!

DEMON D:
(giving up the fight) The contest's over. I'd no doubt her reasoned
rhymes would win it-

FAIRY H:
(sweetly) Well, what, we ask, is life without a touch of poetry in it?

Lighting up to full as all stand to sing 'Hail Poetry'

***At the Hawth Theatre Gala 2000**, lights faded, Thomas Round
stepped forward in a spot to begin 'In Friendship's Name, other
soloists gradually joining in. On closing music, slow fade, and
house tabs in. Lighting to full, tabs opened on intro to 'We leave you
with feelings of pleasure' sung by FULL COMPANY. Curtain calls
followed.*
*(Selected numbers from each opera can be chosen to suit available
singers)*

Principal singers at the Hawth included:
Fairy Harmony: Cynthia Morey
Demon Discord: John Fryatt
*Thomas Round, Kenneth Sandford, Jill Washington, Yvonne Patrick,
Stephen Davis, Helen Landis, Joseph Shovelton, Bruce Graham,
Donald Francke, John Broad.*
Many other members of the old- and new- D'Oyly Carte participated.

Cast of 'Trial by Jury':
The Learned Judge: Donald Francke;
The Plaintiff: Jill Washington;
The Defendant: Joseph Shovelton;
Counsel: Kenneth Sandford;
Usher: John Broad;
Foreman of the Jury: Bruce Graham;
Associate: Alan Barrett.

Actors in the play preceding 'Trial by Jury':
WS Gilbert : Charles Pemberton
Arthur Sullivan: Anthony Herrick
Richard D'Oyly Carte: Michael Simkins

Printed in the United Kingdom
by Lightning Source UK Ltd.
131052UK00001B/85-108/A